A5

MW01502813

30 Days to
Better Organization

A Take-Action Journal

Dancing Lotus Publications

Hartford, CT

Published by Dancing Lotus Publications

Copyright © 2019

DancingLotusPublications.com

ISBN 978-1-7336774-0-0

Dedication

Donna Finocchiaro began her Organizing career in 2004, and can remember organizing as a young girl. She was always inspired by her mother, Virginia Veillette, to whom this book is dedicated.

This is Donna's first book.

Notes

Table of Contents

Insights to Organization

More often than not, my clients feel organization requires large amounts of time or skill. I'm here to inform you this is not true.

We all organize something daily, only we don't recognize the task as such. For instance, loading a dishwasher or placing utensils in a drawer are both organizing-type tasks.

Folding towels or clothing and placing on a shelf or in a drawer are also organizing tasks under the umbrella of doing laundry.

Do you sort your clothing before washing them? This is an organizing skill. If not, give it a try and see how much time you save later.

About This Journal

I have provided you with a tool to help you track your daily organization.

In this journal you will:

- ○ Identify an organizing task each day
- ○ Record learned tasks
- ○ Identify ways to be more organized

Create a habit of journaling at the same time each day or keep this journal with you, close at hand, to record thoughts as they occur.

How to Use This Journal

- ☐ Complete days one through five.
- ☐ Recap those days and celebrate.
- ☐ Tackle the next five days.
- ☐ Evaluate your level of organization.
- ☐ Continue in five day increments throughout this 30-day journey.
- ☐ Notice the changes over time, as you create habits of organization!

Notes

Activity
Pages

Why It's Important to Me to Be Better Organized

_____

_____

_____

_____

_____

_____

_____

My Intentions for Using This Journal

_____

_____

_____

_____

_____

_____

_____

What My Life Will Be Like
When I Am More Organized

_____

_____

_____

_____

_____

_____

_____

The Things I'm Committed to
For Better Organization

_____

_____

_____

_____

_____

_____

_____

The Essence of My Organizing Abilities

What I Love Most About Being Organized

_____

_____

_____

_____

_____

Types of Organizing Projects I Enjoy Most

_____

_____

_____

_____

_____

_____

Here Are Some of My Best Organizing Tips for You

May these tips support you on your journey.

Tip 1: Start small and celebrate your accomplishments.

Tip 2: Set a timer and take hydrating and snack breaks midway.

Tip 3: Break large projects into small pieces.

Tip 4: Work with someone who will inspire you to keep going.

Tip 5: Take on more difficult projects when you are at your best.

Here Are Some of My Best Organizing Tips for You

May these tips support you on your journey.

Tip 6: Stay focused on the task at hand, placing like items together.

Tip 7: Put items that belong elsewhere, into a container for a new task.

Tip 8: With each project, label items as keep, donate, or discard.

Tip 9: Make quick decisions first, handle sentimental items separately.

Tip 10: If the item no longer serves you, let it go!

Notes

Journal
Pages

Day 1 Date: _____

What I Organized Today

_____

_____

_____

_____

_____

_____

Why I Chose This Project

_____

_____

_____

_____

_____

_____

How Working On This Project Made Me Feel

_____

_____

_____

_____

_____

What Challenges I Faced

_____

_____

_____

_____

_____

What I Learned Today

_____

_____

_____

_____

_____

Day 2 Date: _____

What I Organized Today

_____

_____

_____

_____

_____

_____

Why I Chose This Project

_____

_____

_____

_____

_____

_____

_____

How Working On This Project Made Me Feel

_____

_____

_____

_____

_____

What Challenges I Faced

_____

_____

_____

_____

_____

What I Learned Today

_____

_____

_____

_____

Day 3 Date: _____

What I Organized Today

_____

_____

_____

_____

_____

_____

Why I Chose This Project

_____

_____

_____

_____

_____

_____

How Working On This Project Made Me Feel

_____

_____

_____

_____

_____

What Challenges I Faced

_____

_____

_____

_____

_____

What I Learned Today

_____

_____

_____

_____

_____

Day 4 Date: _____

What I Organized Today

_____

_____

_____

_____

_____

_____

Why I Chose This Project

_____

_____

_____

_____

_____

_____

How Working On This Project Made Me Feel

_____

_____

_____

_____

_____

What Challenges I Faced

_____

_____

_____

_____

_____

What I Learned Today

_____

_____

_____

_____

_____

Day 5 Date: _____

What I Organized Today

_____
_____
_____
_____
_____
_____
_____

Why I Chose This Project

_____
_____
_____
_____
_____
_____

How Working On This Project Made Me Feel

_____

_____

_____

_____

_____

What Challenges I Faced

_____

_____

_____

_____

What I Learned Today

_____

_____

_____

_____

Gems from My Journal

Now that you've journaled for five consecutive days, record a gem or two from each day.

Day 1: _____

_____

_____

Day 2: _____

_____

_____

Day 3: _____

_____

_____

Day 4: _____

_____

_____

Day 5: _____

_____

_____

Organized People in My Life

We often learn from the best. Identify people in your life who are especially organized, in a particular area.

Name of Person	Area of Expertise

Notes

Notes

Day 6 Date: _____

What I Organized Today

_____

_____

_____

_____

_____

_____

Why I Chose This Project

_____

_____

_____

_____

_____

_____

_____

How Working On This Project Made Me Feel

_____

_____

_____

_____

_____

What Challenges I Faced

_____

_____

_____

_____

What I Learned Today

_____

_____

_____

_____

Day 7 Date: _____

What I Organized Today

_____

_____

_____

_____

_____

_____

Why I Chose This Project

_____

_____

_____

_____

_____

_____

How Working On This Project Made Me Feel

_____

_____

_____

_____

_____

What Challenges I Faced

_____

_____

_____

_____

What I Learned Today

_____

_____

_____

_____

Day 8 Date: _____

What I Organized Today

_____

_____

_____

_____

_____

_____

Why I Chose This Project

_____

_____

_____

_____

_____

How Working On This Project Made Me Feel

_____

_____

_____

_____

_____

What Challenges I Faced

_____

_____

_____

_____

_____

What I Learned Today

_____

_____

_____

_____

_____

Day 9 Date: _____

What I Organized Today

_____

_____

_____

_____

_____

_____

Why I Chose This Project

_____

_____

_____

_____

_____

_____

How Working On This Project Made Me Feel

_____

_____

_____

_____

_____

What Challenges I Faced

_____

_____

_____

_____

_____

What I Learned Today

_____

_____

_____

_____

_____

Day 10 Date: _____

What I Organized Today

_____

_____

_____

_____

_____

_____

Why I Chose This Project

_____

_____

_____

_____

_____

_____

How Working On This Project Made Me Feel

_____

_____

_____

_____

_____

What Challenges I Faced

_____

_____

_____

_____

_____

What I Learned Today

_____

_____

_____

_____

_____

Gems from My Journal

Take a moment to record five additional gems.

Day 6: _____

_____

_____

Day 7: _____

_____

_____

Day 8: _____

_____

_____

Day 9: _____

_____

_____

Day 10: _____

_____

_____

You've Got This!

I know it's difficult to keep up the pace, but don't stop now.

Here are some words of wisdom to help you along the way.

The *linen closet* is one my favorites.

- ○ Fold the items neatly by type and stack by color, light to dark.
- ○ Fold small towels and wash clothes in half and roll them for easy access.

Your *sock drawer* challenge.

- ○ Do you have unmatched socks? If so, place them in a container to be matched on another day.
- ○ When the missing sock doesn't appear on laundry day, let it go.

Transform your *clothing closet*.

- ○ Hang like items together and by color, light to dark.
- ○ Relocate empy hangers to one side of the closet or bring them to the laundry room.

Notes

Notes

Day 11 Date: _____

What I Organized Today

_____

_____

_____

_____

_____

_____

Why I Chose This Project

_____

_____

_____

_____

_____

_____

How Working On This Project Made Me Feel

_____

_____

_____

_____

_____

What Challenges I Faced

_____

_____

_____

_____

_____

What I Learned Today

_____

_____

_____

_____

_____

Day 12 Date: _____

What I Organized Today

_____

_____

_____

_____

_____

_____

Why I Chose This Project

_____

_____

_____

_____

_____

_____

How Working On This Project Made Me Feel

_____

_____

_____

_____

_____

What Challenges I Faced

_____

_____

_____

_____

What I Learned Today

_____

_____

_____

_____

Day 13 Date: _____

What I Organized Today

_____

_____

_____

_____

_____

_____

Why I Chose This Project

_____

_____

_____

_____

_____

_____

How Working On This Project Made Me Feel

_____

_____

_____

_____

_____

What Challenges I Faced

_____

_____

_____

_____

What I Learned Today

_____

_____

_____

_____

Day 14 Date: _____

What I Organized Today

_____

_____

_____

_____

_____

_____

Why I Chose This Project

_____

_____

_____

_____

_____

_____

How Working On This Project Made Me Feel

_____

_____

_____

_____

_____

What Challenges I Faced

_____

_____

_____

_____

_____

What I Learned Today

_____

_____

_____

_____

_____

Day 15 Date: _____

What I Organized Today

_____

_____

_____

_____

_____

_____

Why I Chose This Project

_____

_____

_____

_____

_____

_____

_____

How Working On This Project Made Me Feel

_____

_____

_____

_____

_____

What Challenges I Faced

_____

_____

_____

_____

_____

What I Learned Today

_____

_____

_____

_____

_____

Gems from My Journal

Take a moment to record five additional gems.

Day 11: _____

_____

_____

Day 12: _____

_____

_____

Day 13: _____

_____

_____

Day 14: _____

_____

_____

Day 15: _____

_____

_____

Evaluate Your Feelings
About Each of the Following

My Time Spent on Organizing

_____

_____

_____

Ability to Change My Thoughts on Organizing

_____

_____

_____

People in My Life Who Are
Especially Organized

_____

_____

_____

Notes

Notes

Day 16 Date: _____

What I Organized Today

_____

_____

_____

_____

_____

_____

Why I Chose This Project

_____

_____

_____

_____

_____

_____

How Working On This Project Made Me Feel

_____
_____
_____
_____
_____

What Challenges I Faced

_____
_____
_____
_____
_____

What I Learned Today

_____
_____
_____
_____
_____

Day 17 Date: _____

What I Organized Today

_____

_____

_____

_____

_____

_____

Why I Chose This Project

_____

_____

_____

_____

_____

_____

How Working On This Project Made Me Feel

_____

_____

_____

_____

_____

What Challenges I Faced

_____

_____

_____

_____

_____

What I Learned Today

_____

_____

_____

_____

_____

Day 18 Date: _____

What I Organized Today

_____
_____
_____
_____
_____
_____

Why I Chose This Project

_____
_____
_____
_____
_____
_____

How Working On This Project Made Me Feel

_____

_____

_____

_____

_____

What Challenges I Faced

_____

_____

_____

_____

_____

What I Learned Today

_____

_____

_____

_____

_____

Day 19 Date: _____

What I Organized Today

_____
_____
_____
_____
_____
_____

Why I Chose This Project

_____
_____
_____
_____
_____
_____

How Working On This Project Made Me Feel

_____

_____

_____

_____

_____

What Challenges I Faced

_____

_____

_____

_____

_____

What I Learned Today

_____

_____

_____

_____

_____

Day 20 Date:_____

What I Organized Today

_____

_____

_____

_____

_____

_____

Why I Chose This Project

_____

_____

_____

_____

_____

_____

How Working On This Project Made Me Feel

_____

_____

_____

_____

_____

What Challenges I Faced

_____

_____

_____

_____

_____

What I Learned Today

_____

_____

_____

_____

_____

Gems from My Journal

Take a moment to record five additional gems.

Day 16: _____

_____

_____

Day 17: _____

_____

_____

Day 18: _____

_____

_____

Day 19: _____

_____

_____

Day 20: _____

_____

_____

Habits Are Forming

The time is now! Start to record changes you are noticing in your organizational abilities.

_____

_____

_____

_____

_____

_____

_____

_____

_____

_____

_____

_____

_____

_____

_____

_____

_____

_____

_____

_____

Notes

Notes

Day 21 Date: _____

What I Organized Today

_____

_____

_____

_____

_____

_____

Why I Chose This Project

_____

_____

_____

_____

_____

_____

How Working On This Project Made Me Feel

_____

_____

_____

_____

_____

What Challenges I Faced

_____

_____

_____

_____

_____

What I Learned Today

_____

_____

_____

_____

_____

Day 22 Date: _____

What I Organized Today

_____
_____
_____
_____
_____
_____

Why I Chose This Project

_____
_____
_____
_____
_____
_____

How Working On This Project Made Me Feel

_____

_____

_____

_____

_____

What Challenges I Faced

_____

_____

_____

_____

_____

What I Learned Today

_____

_____

_____

_____

_____

Day 23 Date: _____

What I Organized Today

_____

_____

_____

_____

_____

_____

Why I Chose This Project

_____

_____

_____

_____

_____

_____

How Working On This Project Made Me Feel

_____

_____

_____

_____

_____

What Challenges I Faced

_____

_____

_____

_____

What I Learned Today

_____

_____

_____

_____

Day 24 Date: _____

What I Organized Today

_____
_____
_____
_____
_____
_____

Why I Chose This Project

_____
_____
_____
_____
_____
_____

How Working On This Project Made Me Feel

_____

_____

_____

_____

_____

What Challenges I Faced

_____

_____

_____

_____

_____

What I Learned Today

_____

_____

_____

_____

_____

Day 25 Date:_____

What I Organized Today

_____

_____

_____

_____

_____

_____

Why I Chose This Project

_____

_____

_____

_____

_____

_____

How Working On This Project Made Me Feel

_____

_____

_____

_____

_____

What Challenges I Faced

_____

_____

_____

_____

_____

What I Learned Today

_____

_____

_____

_____

_____

Gems from My Journal

Take a moment to record five additional gems.

Day 21: _____

_____

_____

Day 22: _____

_____

_____

Day 23: _____

_____

_____

Day 24: _____

_____

_____

Day 25: _____

_____

_____

The Progress I'm Making

Journal the thoughts you are having
about your organizing goals.

_____

_____

_____

_____

_____

_____

_____

_____

_____

_____

_____

_____

_____

_____

_____

_____

_____

Notes

Notes

_____

_____

_____

_____

_____

_____

_____

_____

_____

_____

_____

_____

_____

_____

_____

_____

_____

_____

_____

_____

_____

Day 26 Date: _____

What I Organized Today

_____

_____

_____

_____

_____

_____

Why I Chose This Project

_____

_____

_____

_____

_____

How Working On This Project Made Me Feel

_____

_____

_____

_____

_____

What Challenges I Faced

_____

_____

_____

_____

_____

What I Learned Today

_____

_____

_____

_____

_____

Day 27 Date: _____

What I Organized Today

_____

_____

_____

_____

_____

_____

Why I Chose This Project

_____

_____

_____

_____

_____

_____

How Working On This Project Made Me Feel

_____

_____

_____

_____

_____

What Challenges I Faced

_____

_____

_____

_____

_____

What I Learned Today

_____

_____

_____

_____

_____

Day 28 Date: _____

What I Organized Today

_____

_____

_____

_____

_____

_____

Why I Chose This Project

_____

_____

_____

_____

_____

_____

How Working On This Project Made Me Feel

_____

_____

_____

_____

_____

What Challenges I Faced

_____

_____

_____

_____

What I Learned Today

_____

_____

_____

_____

Day 29 Date: _____

What I Organized Today

_____

_____

_____

_____

_____

_____

Why I Chose This Project

_____

_____

_____

_____

_____

_____

How Working On This Project Made Me Feel

_____

_____

_____

_____

_____

What Challenges I Faced

_____

_____

_____

_____

_____

What I Learned Today

_____

_____

_____

_____

_____

Day 30 Date: _____

What I Organized Today

_____

_____

_____

_____

_____

_____

Why I Chose This Project

_____

_____

_____

_____

_____

_____

How Working On This Project Made Me Feel

_____

_____

_____

_____

_____

What Challenges I Faced

_____

_____

_____

_____

_____

What I Learned Today

_____

_____

_____

_____

_____

Gems from My Journal

Take a moment to record five additional gems.

Day 26: _____

_____

_____

Day 27: _____

_____

_____

Day 28: _____

_____

_____

Day 29: _____

_____

_____

Day 30: _____

_____

_____

Overall Thoughts

Now let's capture your thoughts
about the past 30 days, as follows:

I Am More Organized Today
Than I Was 30 Days Ago Because:

_____

_____

_____

I Am No Longer Afraid to Start an
Organizing Project Because:

_____

_____

_____

My Next Organizing Project Will Be:

_____

_____

_____

Notes

Notes

Notes

Your Inspiring Thoughts

How inspired are you to continue to organize on a daily basis, even if only the smallest of tasks?

Record your thoughts below.

_____

_____

_____

_____

_____

_____

_____

_____

_____

_____

What Are Some of Your Favorite Organizing Tips?

Who Will You Influence to Become More Organized?

- ○ _____
- ○ _____
- ○ _____
- ○ _____
- ○ _____
- ○ _____
- ○ _____
- ○ _____
- ○ _____
- ○ _____
- ○ _____
- ○ _____
- ○ _____
- ○ _____
- ○ _____
- ○ _____

My Favorite Books
About Organizing

- ○ _____
- ○ _____
- ○ _____
- ○ _____
- ○ _____
- ○ _____
- ○ _____
- ○ _____
- ○ _____
- ○ _____
- ○ _____
- ○ _____
- ○ _____
- ○ _____
- ○ _____
- ○ _____
- ○ _____

Organizing Tips
I've Learned

○ _____
○ _____
○ _____
○ _____
○ _____
○ _____
○ _____
○ _____
○ _____
○ _____
○ _____
○ _____
○ _____
○ _____
○ _____
○ _____
○ _____

About Donna

Donna is a Professional Organizer and the owner of Lotus Transitions, where Peace of Mind is her number one priority. She created her company to help navigate the challenges that come with transitioning from one home to another.

Since 2004, Donna has assisted more than one-thousand clients. She loves sharing her organizing skills and industry knowledge with others.

What sets Donna apart is her ability to transfer her lifetime of experience in all areas of her business.

As a professional speaker, Donna has spoken to groups both small and large, from twelve to twelve-hundred.

If you would like Donna to speak to your group, contact her to reserve your space now.

36747566R00062

Made in the USA
Middletown, DE
17 February 2019